THE
FOUR SEASONS
IN POETRY

Some are Covid-Inspired

ERWIN PARENT

THE FOUR SEASONS IN POETRY:
Some are Covid-Inspired
Copyright © 2023 **Erwin Parent**

Because of the dynamic nature of the Internet, any web addresses or links contained in this book may have changed since publication and may no longer be valid. The views expressed in the work are solely those of the author and do not necessarily reflect the views of the publisher, and the publisher hereby disclaims any responsibility for them.

ISBN (Paperback): 978-1-958475-37-9
ISBN (Ebook): 978-1-958475-38-6

Printed in the United States of America.

PROMINENT
BOOKS

5830 E 2nd St, Ste 7000 #9983
Casper, WY 82609
USA

Spring

Summer

Autumn

Winter

CONTENTS

INTRODUCTION

I have always been fascinated by nature—the four seasons, the landscapes, the resilience of the earth after a fire. Even a lowly weed can produce a lovely flower. Nature is poetry in its own way; maybe that is why I have grown to appreciate it so much.

The past year or so, during this once-in-a-lifetime pandemic, we have seen so much distress—people dying worldwide, so much anger, people behaving in strange ways. Some committed suicide; some seniors died from depression, after not being able to have visitors. During this ordeal, I myself was isolated to my room, not able to go out in bad air prompted by local forest fires or bad weather. But my faith in God brought me inspiration I have never felt before. Ideas would come, and I would begin to write what I have seen and felt.

If family members were in a senior facility, they could not be visited indoors. My family joined others, on drive-bys, in long lines of vehicles to drive through the facilities' grounds so we could wave at those inside.

Never, in my eighty-six years of living on planet Earth, have I seen such sadness or anger displayed in many ways.

The book contains some poems written during the Covid-19 pandemic. The pandemic covered the four seasons. Even that brought me inspiration that I can share. These will be commented with Covid-19 Inspired.

My three previous books that have been published by Stratton Press are the following:

1. *Death of a Spouse*
2. *God Has a Plan*
3. *Thank God for You*

I did not start writing poetry until the death of my first wife, Virginia, in 1991. We were married for thirty-five years. It was a way of being able to climb out of the pit of despair that I was in. I have not stopped writing since.

POEMS INSPIRED BY THE CHANGING SEASONS

I was always fascinated by the changing seasons. Since I was brought up in New England, Boston specifically, I saw them firsthand.

Sometimes the season is dry or wetter than usual. Sometimes more brutal than expected. It is sometimes hard to predict. But watching nature adjust was always interesting. The birds adapted, as well as squirrels, foxes, and other species.

Some of my poems have comments on why they were written. I think this is the best way for the reader to see my mindset at the time of writing the poems.

While visiting anywhere no matter what season, I would recommend visiting our Native Americans. They are part of our history. I always loved to watch them dance and to see how they had to live—a wonderful history experience for your children or grandchildren.

At one point, we lived just twenty-five miles from Plymouth, Massachusetts. We would visit Plymouth Plantation there during Thanksgiving. The kids loved it.

SPRING

Spring is so different in many parts of the country. If you normally have snow and cold weather, you may have an early or late spring. Since I have lived in Boston, Massachusetts, and California, I remember seeing flowers peeking through the snow. This year in California, it was an extremely high allergy season; the flowers blossomed early and were everywhere. I've never seen the trees and bushes filled with flowers as I have this past year.

My Wildflower

Walking through woods one day,
Hidden from the sun's warm ray;
Beneath a thick and heavy bower,
I stumbled on a lone wildflower.
Was I the first or only one?
Perhaps not even yet the sun,
That looked upon this beauty rare,
This lovely thing beyond compare.

Tempted though to pluck this flower,
I resisted there with all my power;
To leave this thing of beauty there,
So others this scene could share;
How I would have loved it though,
To take it home and there to show,
To place within my ivory tower,
This rare beauty, my wildflower.

Enticed though to protect and cover,
I wanted to remain and hover,
But knew it needed air and light;
I resisted this with all my might;
It's there today still on my mind,
It's there for someone else to find;
Where it grows beneath the bower,
This beauty rare, my wildflower.

Valentine's Day

What love is can never be changed,
Not even a Covid-19 event can interfere;
A gift neatly wrapped whatever it is,
Is gladly accepted and held ever so dear.

If the love of your life lives very far away,
It is hard fearing that Covid-19 is also there;
But we pray to the same God for support,
Who loves us both and is everywhere.

If you are close to your love visit often,
Together you can appreciate a happy time;
Even with the Covid-19 you're not forced apart,
It is just another mountain here to climb.

Appreciate each other; this is a special day,
It may be like no other day in the future;
Later, looking back, you will appreciate,
That love even in worse times can occur.

Covid-19 Inspired

A Morning Walk

I walked a wooded path one springtime morn
Everything seeming new and freshly born;
The earthen floor wet with heavy dew
Came to life in an orchestrated cue.

The very air I breathed was crisp and clean,
Life began to stir, though still unseen;
The dew formed in puddles on the leaves,
And beaded on the web the spider weaves.

The trees, their cloistered shadows fled,
Now formed a vaulted ceiling overhead;
A caterpillar crossed a fallen leaf,
A crocus peeking out from beneath.

Sun filtering rays, the darkness broke
Warming the bowers in its cloak;
A raven broke the silence with a shriek,
Allowing its inner hunger to speak.

The sparrow gathered items for its nest,
A robin flared its reddened breast,
Squirrels revisited their hiding places,
Chipmunks rubbing sleepy morning faces.

I'll walk this way again another time,
To hear the many birds in chorus chime,
And seek peace within this holy tower
Finding rest beneath this sacred bower.

Placing Flowers at My Headstone

When placing flowers at my headstone,
I request they be red, white, and blue;
I want to first honor our flag,
And then all that we hold so true.

One a bluebell, and give me not a few,
It's a reminder to never hang our head;
Keep our head held high and be proud
Like many of my brothers here dead.

White carnations for innocence lost,
A reminder of a life unfulfilled;
All the things that could have been,
Like our farmland lying untilled.

Bright red roses for lives unlived,
Of our families never seen again;
A wife and children we never had,
Like the fate of an abandoned train.

If you do these simple things for me,
You will my faith and honor renew;
My eyes will be focused on heaven,
At attention I'll be saluting you.

Flowers Unmasked

The flowers blooming are beautiful this year,
All this despite the pandemic's trending fear;
The very next time I pray to God I will ask,
Why are the beautiful smiles behind the mask?

The sun is out, and birds are busy right here,
The flowers brightly shine and the air is clear.
On Easter celebration, we sang He has risen,
Why must we feel we are still in prison?

The flowers grow in bunches; they have no fear,
We have to distance, saying, "Don't come near."
The very next time I pray to God I will ask,
Why are the beautiful smiles behind the mask?

Covid-19 Inspired

Easter

Celebrating a Covid-19 Easter, but He is still risen,
Even our flowered cross looks more beautiful;
Our church is closed, but we are together outside,
The music filling our hearts and is never dull.

Not another Easter like this ever again we state,
This Covid-19 has penetrated our lives worldwide;
The hymns we heard outside are not the same,
Next year hopefully we will hear them inside.

Lord, come and help us roll this Covid-19 away,
Just as the stone was moved from Jesus's tomb;
We can do this, we say, but we need your help,
Come and help us erase this thought of gloom.

Happy Easter next year in our church we sing,
Come and listen; help us roll this Covid-19 away;
He has risen; let us never forget these words,
Come and help us have a free and happy day.

Covid-19 Inspired

On the Other Side of the Mirror

The pandemic rages on; we wonder if we will survive,
The isolation is awful friends nor family do we see;
The children play on, ignorant of what is happening,
We worry about neighbors, but where can we flee?

On the other side of the mirror, the wind still blows,
The flowers still blossom and greet the morning sun;
The birds still sing and go through their daily routine,
The grass is watered, and many start their morning run.

Anger seems everywhere in homes and without,
Businesses are closed and many now are jobless;
Children start school at home some using laptops,
Depression dominates us all the future is hopeless.

On the other side of the mirror the world goes on,
Shopping and restaurants even church for some;
Planning vacations from work many trips to take,
Life is good with many blessings we are overcome.

Covid-19 Inspired

Aspirations

I will aspire; I will reach for the sky,
Nothing will hinder my earthly quest;
I will do more than dream, I will try,
You will see me perform my very best.

I will aspire; I will keep an open mind,
Nothing will I withhold from thought;
I will do more than seek, I will find,
I will apply in life all that I am taught.

I will aspire; I will bare my very soul,
Nothing will stifle my inner passion;
I will do more than achieve my goal,
I will view the world with compassion.

I will aspire; I will have an open heart,
No one will I withhold from my love;
I will do more than care, I will impart,
All negative things I will rise above.

Covid-19 Inspired

I Will Bring You Flowers

When the day is done some early Spring Day,
I will gather flowers from our garden for you;
I hope it will be a surprise that you didn't see,
It will always be better when you never knew.

I know that a flower display can make your day,
But I can't pick too many, or they will be gone;
But I love to find any way to make you smile,
I can always say the Covid-19 made me do it a Con.

This year the flowers are so many filling a bush,
The blossoms are many, which will keep it full;
So when they are picked it seems untouched,
But I'll keep it going the displays chock-full.

When the bush is empty, you can yell at me,
I'll say but all those lovely smiles I got to see;
You will say you didn't have to pick them all,
And I will say the Covid-19 kicked me in the knee.

Covid-19 Inspired

SUMMER

The summer, no matter where you are, is generally hot. Because of the Covid-19, many parks and playgrounds are empty. The homeless are forced to move to new locations so cleanup can be performed. In Boston, Massachusetts, during the summer, it was hot and very humid. Going to the shore, especially Cape Cod, was one way to get relief.

When we move to Los Angeles, California, area, we loved exploring; it was all new. Driving to Lake Tahoe was a wonderful experience.

Thank You God Once Again

The pandemic rages on yet the flowers still blossom,
We wonder in these difficult times will we survive;
In the many events during my lifetime I prayed,
In the end I too blossomed and here I am alive.

The isolation is unbearable yet the wind still blows,
Outside no one can be seen but our flag will wave;
All the years that I have dwelled under your wings,
Prayerful times spend on my knees and you forgave.

The fear that overcomes us yet the sun still shines,
Anger seems everywhere raging now and then;
We may have been here before in another time,
We are now able to say thank you God once again.

Depression dominates us all yet the birds still sing,
We hide our thoughts not knowing bad from good;
We worry about family members those near and far,
Hoping they are well and have this Covid-19 withstood.

Then when it is over and our normal life returns,
See friends and family and at church we say amen;
We now can feel blessed and once again survived,
We are now able to say thank you God once again.

Covid-19 Inspired

A Garden

A garden is a place where hope grows,
Where Begonias wax and Shamrocks close,
Where Mushrooms hide and Lilies pose
And hope is harvested from endless rows.

A garden is a place where wishes bloom,
Where Roses bud and Sunflowers loom,
Where Irises stand like stiffened grooms
And wishes nurtured lift the gloom.

A garden is a place where peace prevails,
Where Bluebells ring and Cornstalks hail,
Where Mums are hushed and Daisies pale
And peace withstands the fiercest gale.

Just for Me

During the pandemic, we were isolated, unable to go out,
Also forest fires with smoke so thick we couldn't see;
There on a bush outside my window grew a flower,
Growing only on the inside of the bush it was just for me.

The birds usually high in the tree were now moving lower,
The smoke and ashes covering what they ate with debris;
Their tweets and songs filling the air with lovely sounds,
Hearing this music not usually there it was just for me.

As we go through life and think back at important events,
I could remember the unique things I could never foresee;
Somehow the good Lord had placed them in sequence,
That lined these incidents so they could be just for me.

The loves of our life we met often in unusual happenings,
We never knew they were preplanned and meant to be;
Partnerships lasting a lifetime and sometimes even beyond,
Little did I know that somehow she was there just for me.

Covid-19 Inspired

Moon over Modesto

The Moon over Modesto is shining bright this year,
It's on the Weeping Willows where they shed a tear;
It's lighting up the pathways where the lovers stroll,
It's shining on the Buttercups upon the grassy knoll.

The Moon over Modesto is glowing bright this year,
It's comforting the homeless and things they hold dear;
It's blessing the nest of the Western Meadowlark.
It's lighting up the playgrounds in every city park.

The Moon over Modesto is shining bright this year,
It's consoling the helpless cringing in fear;
It's shining on fields where crops used to grow,
It's lighting up the hillsides where the flowers blow.

It's glowing on the fruit and nuts growing nearby,
It's shining on the waterways that are getting dry;
It's cherishing the blind and those who cannot hear,
The Moon over Modesto is shining bright this year.

The Crosses

The bravest are those who stormed the beach at Normandy,
Now lie in rows of endless crosses as far as eye can see;
Their hopes and dreams are shattered and lie unfulfilled,
The families left at home whose futures have been stilled.

They are listening now to the beat of a different drummer,
They are marching side by side in an infinite number;
No rank nor race nor gender will separate them now,
We will never fight again the weary world will vow.

Where is the peace? Where has that promise gone we ask?
It held such promise it seemed like such a simple task;
It must come from within each heart to end all warfare,
It is the task of humankind; it is our own cross to bear.

The bravest are those who stormed the beach at Normandy,
Now lie in rows of endless crosses as far as eye can see;
Their hopes and dreams are buried there where they lay,
The families left at home never had a homecoming day.

As Long

As long as I have breath
I will inhale the free air,
Fought for and won by heroes
Those who dare and repair.

As long as I can hear
I will listen for the cries,
Of the innocent child
And sympathize.

As long as I can see
I will look for the good,
Found deep in mankind
Not always understood.

As long as I can speak
I will voice only healing
Words of comfort to,
Those who are unfeeling.

As long as my heart beats
I will throw out my chest,
Each time I see our flag
And pray for the unblessed.

Summer Anger in the Streets

The innocents are attacked all within sight,
Beaten for no reason, falling to the ground;
Crowds moving to the next street for more,
Hospitals overwhelmed as many are found.

When nights are dark there is anger still,
The crowds keep everyone nearby awake;
Beyond the curfew often put in place,
Many in fear are huddled and begin to shake.

Fear keeps people in at night with lights out,
Hiding within the darkness of their home;
Seniors living alone are the hardest hit,
Who will help thoughts start to roam.

This isolation for all has a terrible effect,
I hope no other summer will be like this;
Once in a lifetime is enough for me,
I will look far ahead and pray for bliss.

Covid-19 Inspired

Independence Day

We are free hopefully from this pandemic,
We can't let it keep us locked up for long;
Our nation is strong it members unique,
God Bless America is still our loving song.

We have fought our way to reach this point,
So many of our Veterans are in their graves;
Those many families losing their loved ones,
We stand proud; our nation's flag still waves.

We can't let this pandemic take our freedom,
Or limit our duties needed and used so long;
We will survive; we will rise to the occasion,
We will be tough; and we will also be strong.

This will be our future history in the making,
All of our American family will be proud;
We will march forward as we have before,
We will sing God Bless America very loud.

Covid-19 Inspired

Summer Storms

The clouds and rain come with summer storms,
Will continue through the hot weather this year;
But when it's over we get that beautiful rainbow,
That smile that comes from God and is ear to ear.

The rain will water a needy and fertile ground,
We hope it washes the Covid-19 away from us;
We hope it provides food for many in need,
We pray it helps the many who are homeless.

We pray the storms do not damage many homes,
It's always hard when this happens but we look;
Always want to reach out and try to help others,
The Covid-19 may have our thought but we cook.

Let the Rainbow be the smile that makes your day,
We know that Covid-19 won't be around here forever;
Rain go away but please come back another day,
Bring the rainbow with you that's what we prefer.

Covid-19 Inspired

I Saw a Gull

There one day along the shore,
I saw a Gull begin to soar;
It sailed on winds with grace and ease,
It soared so high upon this breeze
I wished right there before I die
That I could learn one day to fly.

Imagine if this could be true,
I'd lift myself into the blue
And catch a brisk and steady gale
And off to somewhere else I'd sail,
Over problems seeming great
I'd never fret arriving late.

I wonder if this Gull I saw,
Wishes he could change the law;
And drive the car that I was in
Screech around that last hairpin
Passing cars and trucks at will
Down the road and up the hill.

Maybe it would be best,
If we could just leave the rest
To those who think and mull;
I wonder though about that Gull
You think this envy he does wield
Making a mess on my windshield?

Autumn

The autumn in New England is always beautiful, attracting many tourists. To stay where it is cool and to see the beauty of the changing leaves are wonderful. Many tours take place in New England during this time. The autumn leaves displayed are incredible.

One memorable event for me was the hurricane of 1938. It came up the coast and passed through Massachusetts, New Hampshire, and on into Canada. I lived in Massachusetts at the time the wind recorded was 121 mph, with gusts as high as 186 mph. I remember going outside the next morning, and every tree on the street was down, not one left standing.

Nightfall

Shadows lengthen on the walk, and light begins to darken,
Sleepy night beasts start to stir and to the noises hearken;
Fullest blossoms start to close to spend the night at rest,
Mother birds collect their young to settle in their nests;
Silly moths begin to flutter around the lighted porches,
Fireflies take to empty fields to light their little torches.

Bats around the belfry fly to test their radar beams,
Bullfrogs start their grunt along the running streams;
Moonbeams settle on the lea and other earthly places,
Families sit round the fireplace to see each other's faces;
Trees begin a gentle sway amid the cooling breezes,
Dogs and cats will settle down wherever it pleases.

Halloween

Everyone masked not just the trick-or-treaters,
What has the Covid-19 done to mar this event;
Many of our homes are not hosting this year,
We wonder where all the spooky kids went.

A few local events are being held here this year,
We used to take pictures of all the cute kids;
The blank pages will be a reminder next year,
Not much face painting this year on the eyelids.

The neighborhoods are quiet this year so sad,
Everyone wants to protect all the children;
This is important and is part of the history,
We will remember and share now and then.

"Trick or treat." All the kids learned to say.
We will look forward to next year to hear;
Hope the families record this happening.
It is a sad but memorable event this year.

Covid-19 Inspired

A Mighty Oak

If I could pick what I would be,
A mighty Oak tree would you see;
Tiny seed from where I lie,
I'd push my branches to the sky
And poke my roots into the ground,
Until some moisture could be found.

Birds would nest within my arms
And teach their young to fly unharmed;
Squirrels my acorns would they raid,
And lovers picnic in my shade;
On stormy, darkened, moonless night
I'd offer rest to flocks in flight.

Standing weathered, gnarled, and bold,
I'd offer more when I am old;
My sturdy wood will build a house,
Warm children's hands, the cat and mouse;
Dropping acorns when I die,
I'd push more branches to the sky.

Covid-19-Free Leaves

Leaves are now dropping from the sky,
Lying on the ground in a colorful bed;
Squirrels hopping all around for food,
Acorns under the orange, yellow, and red.

Birds are missing all the fallen leaves,
None are hanging over their head;
The birds will move to a new shelter,
Away from the orange, yellow, and red.

The shorter days will soon be here,
Leading us to colder days we dread;
Cool breezes change the tree leaves,
From green to orange, yellow, and red.

Covid-19 Inspired

No Place

There is no place large enough to contain this God of mine,
There is no spot remote where His light doesn't shine;
There is no cathedral any place that can hold Him within,
There is no transgression bad enough to never pardon sin;
There is no church or spire reaching heaven anywhere,
There is no place we need to go to feel His loving care.

I can feel His presence on Yosemite's valley floor,
I can pray to Him in secret behind my closet door;
I can see His innocence in a newborn baby's eyes,
I can sense His presence in the blue of autumn skies;
I can hear His power in the summer thunderstorms,
I can smell His breath in a million flowering forms.

I can taste His sweetness in the nectar of His fruit,
I can hear His harmony in a straining golden flute;
I can see His beauty in the Aurora Borealis,
I can touch His richness in the deepest forest palace;
I can feel His influence upon the ocean brine,
There is no place large enough to contain this God of mine.

Thoughts

During this pandemic we hear children playing,
Nothing can ever silence this true blessing;
We hear dogs barking the Covid-19 is not at fault,
The isolations help I even get to go out fishing.

The autumn leaves are falling all around,
I worry about our neighbors all unseen,
Someday when this is over we will visit,
We will then share on whom did we lean.

Lovers remain in the home waiting it out,
They are without masks it seems so right;
Hopefully they are protected and will be OK,
Looking to the blessings of the morning light.

We worry about family some not nearby,
How are they coping through these days;
The elderly are the most vulnerable,
We hope they stayed within the sun's rays.

Covid-19 Inspired

Thanksgiving

The Pilgrims years ago landed at Plymouth Rock,
Glad that they had no Covid-19 to deal with then;
This year we had our turkey but fewer family,
They will come to see us we don't know when.

All across the country many families could not fly,
It's good we could find means to see them online;
Covid-19 has changed the plans of so many this year,
We pray for all affected that next year will be fine.

The Covid-19 did not change the taste of our turkey,
We prayed for all holding hands before we ate;
This holiday will go down in history a life event,
We will all remember this as a very solemn date.

Just as the Pilgrims were grateful for this day,
We too knowing it may never happen again;
Stay strong and don't let Covid-19 rule your life,
Keeping our faith as the Pilgrims we will win.

Covid-19 Inspired

Walking in the Moonlight

Walking in a city park beneath a lighted moon,
Holding hands with my love not a word to say;
Covid-19 has us out again from isolation inside,
We'll walk this way again we hope and pray.

The quiet evening with autumn smells in the air,
Not many out this night walking all are masked;
The stars are bright the many birds are silent,
How long can this Covid-19 remain? We both asked.

Cooling breezes begin to travel through the park,
Up and down the walks among the empty benches;
Birds will settle in their nests trying to keep warm,
The homeless looking in at us from the park fences.

We'll come this way another time hopefully soon,
We pray that God will keep us safe so we can;
We worry about family and friends near and far,
We pray that God will give them a helping hand.

Covid-19 Inspired

Storm with a Twist

The Autumn storms sometimes have Tornadoes,
Some are fiercer than others here previously;
I wish one would come to take this Covid-19 away,
Send it spinning off into space quite noisily.

The Autumn storms can be very wet and long,
Flooding is a real issue we have to deal with;
Sometimes rescuing people who are trapped,
With this Covid-19 its reality will not be a myth.

Soon the sky will be cloudless here again,
The winds will diminish and we see the stars;
The flooding will recede and return to normal,
We will be able to move around with our cars.

We pray that God will help us survive this year,
So many have lost family members all around;
Help us God to recognize this as only one event,
And that by keeping our faith we will all rebound.

Covid-19 Inspired

Hurricane

The storm is coming from the south very soon,
Along a coastal path that changes every hour;
We follow what we can watching local news,
We worry about falling trees and losing power.

We hope it blows this nasty Covid-19 away forever,
Never to return we say please never to return;
The winds will blow all night as we try to sleep,
The rain will fall all night floods are the concern.

Where do all the birds go during the heavy rain,
As well as the other creatures living here outside;
I'm sure they'll find a place where they can go,
It will be a new place where they can go and hide.

For a storm to cover the same area is very rare,
Perhaps another will come this way some year;
We'll have to wait and see if that ever happens,
Hopefully no Covid-19 will never ever come near.

Covid-19 Inspired

WINTER

Winter in the northern states is always cold. I remember in Boston, Massachusetts, one year, the temperature during the whole month of February never got above zero. Having a snowy Christmas was normal. I remember joining other members of our church and going to sing Christmas carols at someone's home. Many seniors and disabled were unable to get out, and we brought them gifts. A great experience for our children.

We moved to California in the '70s. It was a new experience for us. We could drive to the snow or stay close to the shore areas.

Footprints in the Snow

Footprints in the snow I wonder where they go?
Should I follow or venture out to make my own?
I could follow for a while just check it out,
Then I'll forge new prints as I venture out alone.

Footprints in the snow I wonder where they go?
Are they headed home to a nice warm fire?
After walking in the cold for such a long time,
That's where I would head when I begin to tire.

Footprints in the snow I wonder where they go?
Are they venturing out for an early morning stroll?
Perhaps they are on the hunt for game they can track,
Or are they more like me out to fill an empty soul?

Footprints in the snow I wonder where they go?
Lovers on a morning trip to enjoy the outdoors?
This Covid-19 can't just keep us locked up inside;
Are they expressing their right or just goers?

Footprints in the snow I wonder where they go?
I won't follow them anymore I'll go it on my own,
I'll get to see new fallen snow where none have been;
I'll get to see the places where yet no sun has shone.

Covid-19 Inspired

Hidden Beauty

Where do Poppies go when winter comes?
How can such beauty hide itself like this?
Blowing winter winds its petal numbs,
And dreams begin of springtime's sunny kiss.

Where do Poppies go when winter comes?
Do they reflect on inner-selves and plan?
Might we ask the same of Hyacinths and Mums?
Do they dream of warm spring rain and tans?

Where do Poppies go when winter comes?
Are they preparing fields that run for miles?
Await the bees that kiss and hums,
And glowing heavenwards proudly smiles?

The Churches Are Closed

The churches are closed but my faith is not,
All the pews inside are empty and cold;
The pandemic rages on people want to pray,
But we have to wait to open we are told.

The church is closed but my Bible is open,
You can't shut down blessings received;
The Bible stories cover many centuries,
This is one that will be greatly believed.

The church is closed but my heart is open,
Showing compassion to those we see;
Praying for the many we hear about,
Praying strongly this pandemic will flee.

The church is closed but my eyes are open,
I see goodness well beyond all the evil;
The Father is watching he knows all,
He will provide what we need for a refill.

Covid-19 Inspired

The Birds Adjust

As the pandemic rages on and on,
Birds adjust to finding food;
The playgrounds and parks are empty,
Once happy now in a different mood.

Birds once seen outside my home,
Are no longer there and are missed;
Probably exploring places in the snow,
When this ends they will have a list.

The birds are unafraid of people masked,
Perhaps it's something they don't notice;
When this is over and we get back to normal,
It is something they will all just dismiss.

Covid-19 Inspired

Snow in the Mountains

Snow in the mountains will be wild this year,
Looks like Covid-19 will have no effect at all;
It will rest on the many trees just as before,
When the wind picks up the snow will fall.

Ice on the ponds will be thicker this year,
The fish beneath will feel very secure;
When this Covid-19 is over and it's all gone,
It will be only in our memory just a blur.

Two hikers holding hands walking ahead,
Isolation forced them out to be together;
Covid-19 can have no effect on any lovers,
Togetherness the key in this cold weather.

At night the silence penetrates the darkness,
No creatures moving here or making sounds;
Perhaps they too feel an inner love right now,
No food now to fill them with extra pounds.

Covid-19 Inspired

Christmas

Our Christmas tree is all decorated now,
The shiny balls and lights are all aglow;
Covid-19 has had no effect that we can see,
Baby Jesus is in the manger down below.

Christmas carols are sung now outside,
The music brings comfort to our hearts:
The star that led the wise men from afar,
Shines overhead the celebration starts.

Oh Mother Mary God bless your son,
A very special child we will all learn;
As we go through life we remember,
To heed our inner soul at every turn.

The families now with love abounding,
The seasonal love lights up the room;
We feel the warmth of this love inside,
Like Jesus felt in his Mother's womb.

Covid-19 Inspired

Winter Walks in the Moonlight

Steps upon the new snow now on the ground,
Venturing out of isolation into the Covid-19 air;
Holding hands with my love feeling very free,
In the moonlight shining bright we do not care.

Nothing can limit our effort or hold us back,
The cold air and warm coats keeping us well;
The stars are shining bright in this cold air,
We will have a happy and lovely story to tell.

A warm fireplace waiting for us to return,
The cold boots and gloves will be put away;
Our memory will be filled with this Covid-19,
But our trust in God will complete our day.

Covid-19 Inspired

Love and Snowstorms

The winter snow storms travel through many states,
Sometimes they last for hours leaving huge drifts;
Many must stay inside where it is warm and safe,
With Covid-19 here it seems we are isolated and adrift.

It is the kind of storm I would wish for to be with you,
We would be happy and warm by this fireplace;
Music would be playing maybe a sweet dance or two,
I loved holding and looking into your beautiful face.

Transportation is at a standstill many are marooned,
The motels are filled with people unable to continue;
The snow is piling high hopefully everyone has food,
How Covid-19 is reacting to all of this we have no clue.

I don't want to wait for another storm to see you,
Continuing on without you for me is hard to handle;
Can we make a storm decision and connect for real?
I cannot live without seeing those eyes by our candle.

Covid-19 Inspired

Our Christmas Tree

We take one fir tree from forest green,
Where it grew quietly, strong and serene,
We place it in the midst of our humble home,
The sun no more will shine upon its dome;
Decorate it with things shining bright,
Add some glitter and also some light;
Then with our hearts overflowing with glee,
Drink in the beauty of our Christmas tree.

If we could share this wondrous sight,
With earthly souls in the direst plight;
What gift of ours could we possibly share,
To lessen their pain or load of care?
We could gather together gifts of worth,
Wrap it neatly with our lives of mirth;
And place it there where all can see,
Somewhere beneath our Christmas tree.

No perfumed gifts from Parisian nights,
No flowery fragrance wrapped in white,
No scent from places we could never guess,
Can match one thing that we possess;
If we could capture the essence of our love,
Poured in a bottle, add peaceful dove:
We can place this gift from you and me
Beneath the branches of our Christmas tree.

Can we add to it peace of a Bethlehem night?
Lead those in darkness with star shining bright?
Can we feed the hunger with our affluence here?
Or bring to the inn those huddled in fear?
Can we silence the hate as shepherds their flock?
Lead those tossed on oceans to finally dock?
If we can do all of this what a world it would be,
Sharing this beauty of our Christmas tree.

New Year

A New Year is starting what can we leave behind,
What are the things that we don't want to bring;
Somehow we'll find a way so it won't be missed,
We just have to adjust to living without the thing.

A New Year is starting what can we start doing,
Something that will improve our life somehow;
Helping us to improve our living conditions,
Something new maybe it will work for now.

Covid-19 is one we won't miss; it caused problems,
Hope it doesn't find its way into our New Year;
Yes we can live without it we sure have before,
Imagine going through each day with no fear.

A New Year is upon us I hope it will bring blessings,
I can't wait to receive the blessings pour it on me;
I know already that it will make changes to my life,
Improvements are what's on my list all I hope to see.

Covid-19 Inspired

www.ingramcontent.com/pod-product-compliance
Lightning Source LLC
Chambersburg PA
CBHW051557120626
46551CB00013B/1563